This book belongs to:

PARK PARTY!

MIMI JONES

Dedicated to Delilah, Avalon, and Levi.

ISBN 978-1-958985-23-6

www.joeysavestheday.com

A Mimi Book

Let's go to the park today.

Let's throw a party at the park!

PARTY TIME

Let's plunge headfirst into a sugary mountain of cupcakes and unleash our inner party animals!

Let's dash and frolic at the park like a couple of happy squirrels!

having fun

Let's soar on the swings like
we're flying into the sunset!

Let's take a wild ride down the slide!

Let's bounce on the see-saw and
take our friendship to new heights!

Hop on the bouncy horse and
let's ride into the giggle-fest!

Let's unleash our inner monkeys on the jungle gym!

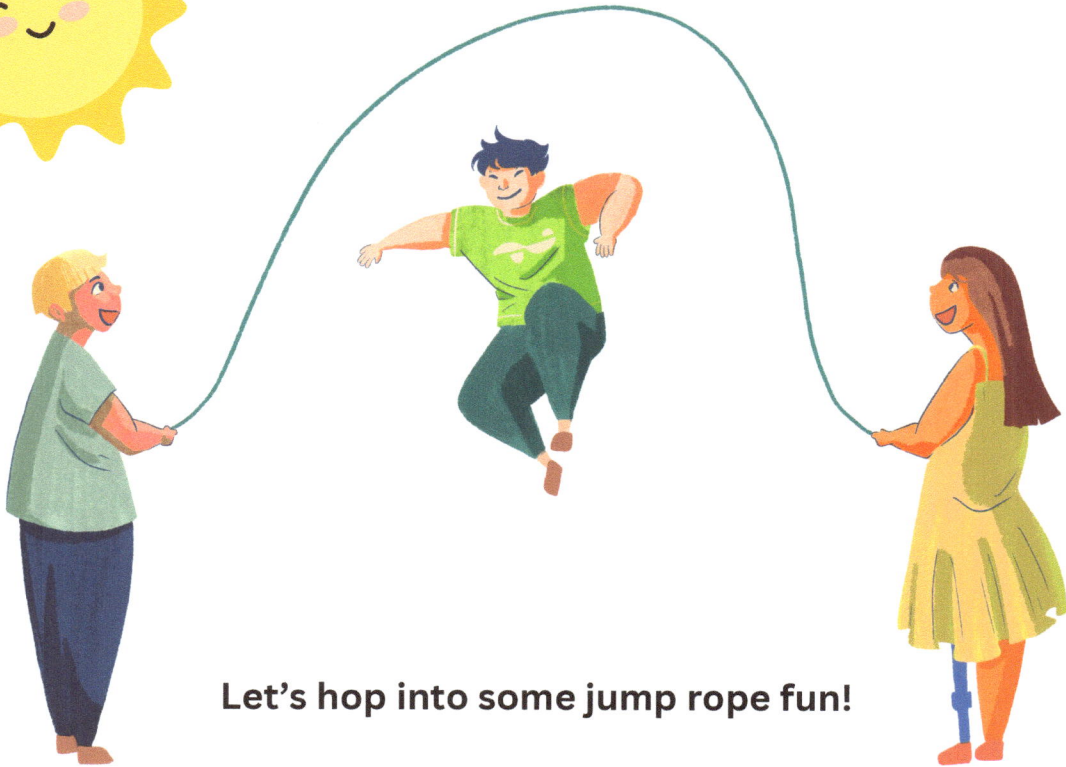

Let's hop into some jump rope fun!

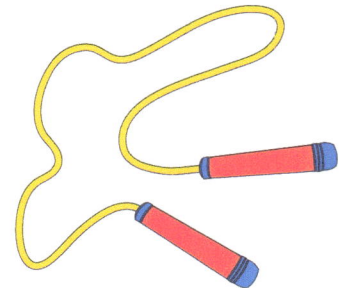

Let's jump into some hopscotch fun!

Let's play on the merry-go-round
and let the fun begin!

Sandbox

Let's dive into the sandbox shenanigans!

Let's read a book at the park.

Ready or not, here we go—let's
dive into a game of hide and seek!

Let's dive into a wild game of tag!

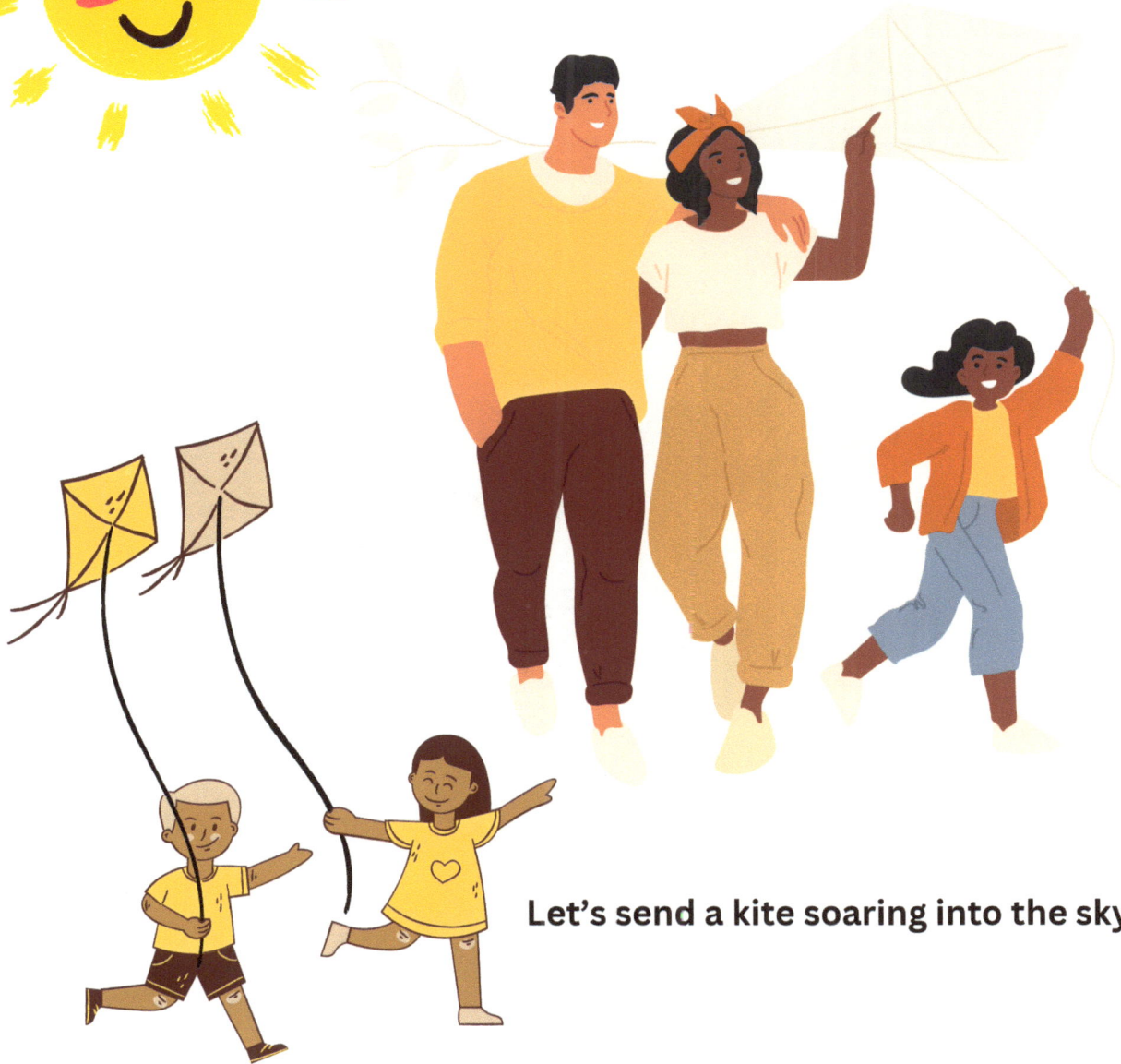

Let's send a kite soaring into the sky!

Let's shoot some hoops and slam dunk our way to fun!

HOOPS

Let's unleash our inner champions
and throw some frisbee fun!

Let's embark on a bug safari!

Let's spin into some
hula hooping fun!

Let's recruit Mom or Dad to give us a turbo boost on the swing!

BaA!

Let's scale the epic climbing wall and channel our inner mountain goats!

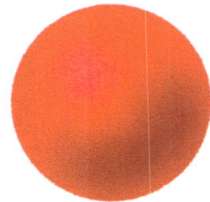

Let's dive into a game of four square madness!

Let's throw down a picnic party!

Let's roll into park escapades on two
wheels or perhaps four—let the fun begin!

Let's stroll down the trail and soak up some nature vibes.

Let's turn our park into a trash-free zone after the party!

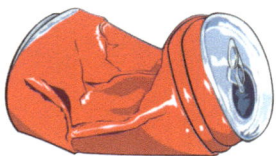

I hope you enjoyed the Park Party book! Remember to stay close to your parents during any park party and avoid strangers.

www.ingramcontent.com/pod-product-compliance
Lightning Source LLC
Chambersburg PA
CBHW060838270326
41933CB00002B/126